# Early Praise for Garland of Grace

## Sitting with the Dying Sun

✷

"Reverend Dr. Nancy Ash's new endeavor, *Garland of Grace*, is her continuous effort to spiritually elevate the minds of the masses and the unity of the sexes. She is a true spiritual giant."

— **Chandra Shekhar,** Rishi DBL Acharya

"Nancy Ash's poetry is gorgeous and such a delight to read—she has a great gift for inner listening. Her latest poems, *Garland of Grace*, are like direct sips of divine nectar from the Goddess. Each time I read one, I feel replenished and renewed from a deep source of wisdom. While poetry books are often not easy to read, don't avoid this one, it is."

— **Claire Sierra, MA,** author of *The Magdalene Path - Awaken the Power of Your Feminine Soul* and Chief Creative Officer of BlissBreakthrough.com

"*Garland of Grace* stirs the wind of your soul to the eternal dance of the feminine attributes. Just let its music take you there ... a quiet place of remembering the power of the sacred feminine heart embrace."

— **Nathalie Campeau, MD,** author of *The Emerging Heart*

"Nancy Ash has given a beautiful poetic voice to Indwelling Divinity of the Sacred Mother and the Sacred Father, the inextricable Truth of Divine Presence… Oneness. The weaving of these melodic words, emerging from the *Via Creativa* Consciousness, create a vibrational tapestry that has brought peace, comfort, and great joy to me. May you find these blessings here, too."

— **Rev. Linda Marie Nelson, DD, PhD,** Abbess, Order of Shekinah Ruha Community

"This book of poems is well-crafted, an introspective masterpiece."

— **D. Joseph LaRon,** writer, producer, director of *The Missionary's Position*

"It is understood by all that poetry is good for the soul. How much more potent for us that Ash's work is directly addressing our innermost Self. "

— **Dr. Nancy North, DC,** author of *Success: Motivational Coloring Education*

"*Garland of Grace* flows like a river of beauty—peaceful, pristine, and powerful—and carries the reader from birth to birth. This book will bless your soul."

— **Ron Brunk,** Nashville songwriter and author of *Mystery Diseases and Me*

"The collection of poems in *Garland of Grace* touched my soul deeply...may your soul be touched as well."

— **Charlotte McGinnis,** Spiritual Leader of The Namaste Center and co-author of *A Golf Course in Miracles*

"In *Garland of Grace: Sitting with the Dying Sun*, the Reverend Dr. Nancy Ash has brought the experiential Human quest for the transcendent reality of the Divine Presence into clear and imminent focus using a broad spectrum of lenses. Drawing on a diverse range of traditions and experiences, both old and new, Dr. Ash has articulated the perennial journey of spiritual exploration and given us some landmarks that we may have missed along the way. Her reflections urge us to look in places many of us prefer not to go, from fear of finding the Ultimate treasures we know are there. *Garland of Grace: Sitting with the Dying Sun* speaks in the language that needs no interpreter but silence. Dr. Ash gets our attention and radically invites us to listen with the Divinely tuned ear of the Human heart. *Garland of Grace: Sitting with the Dying Sun* is a masterpiece of realized spirituality, perhaps even closing in on the precincts of Sacred Literature."

— **The Right Rev. Jack Stafford, PhD,** Bishop, The
    Progressive Episcopal Church


"From the depths of her soul, Nancy Ash brings to life the wonders of nature, the incredible aspects of being and the blessings that abound through the eyes of a true poet. Travel with her through blossoming words, through images drawn in the imagination and from desires that dance in the moonlight. Revel in the beauty that begs to be explored in our bountiful and magnificent earth as Nancy delivers a full cup of elixir for every curious and hungry soul."

— **Liz Sterling,** radio talk show host and author of
    *Behind the Scenes: Celebrity Interviews and Inspiring*
    *Life Lessons*

"... As The Noble Lady, The Mistress, The Temptress, The Black Madonna, The Cosmic Mother... The Sacred Feminine of Infinity in ALL her glorious forms from all-over, Nancy's supreme gift to connect with The One, and her uncanny, potent and breath-taking flair to put this into words and voice always compels one to halt... to sit ... and to listen. Her explanations of the mystical terms used in this awesome collection of poetry affirms Nancy as a heart-centered mystic and veteran teacher of the sacred ancient ways that she is. Ah! *Garland of Grace* is a real and beautiful treasure and an honest and timeless companion on the road of re-turning and Be-Coming: uBu-ntu!"

— **Anna-Mari Pieterse,** Daughter of Africa - Land of the Sun, Humanitysteam.org

"Nancy's poems, musings of devotion, whisk the reader to hushed, silken temples of the East, majestic deserts and mountains of the West and all sacred places between. This is a book to savor in moments of reflection and when it's time to spark the Soul."

— **Rev. Shellie Enteen**, radio host of *Esoterically Speaking* and author of *Journey to the Meaning of Love*

"*Garland of Grace: Sitting with the Dying Sun* swept me along into mindset of ancient memories. Each poem touched a different place of dancing with impermanence and yet embracing the oneness simultaneously. Each poem spoke to me of a deep connection that the author has to her first-hand mystical knowledge of the Source in its many beautiful expressions. I was transported to

Chaco Canyon, to ancient rituals, and to a deep love of Spirit that honors the value of sitting with a dying sun. As with any poem that touches you, I will not see the world the same way again. Thank you for the connection and the wisdom."

— **Rev. Cathy Haven Howard**, author of *Spirit Expression for Everyone* and *Living the Truth of Who You Are*

✦

# Garland of Grace

## Sitting with the Dying Sun

A Poetry Collection
Celebrating Re-Emergence
of the
Sacred Feminine

Also by Nancy Ash

*Doing a 360*
*Turning Your Life Around to Follow Soul's Purpose*

Visit www.Doinga360.com

# Garland of Grace

## Sitting with the Dying Sun

Reverend Dr. Nancy Ash

To

~ All Women ~

All Men

Especially, You

# Garland of Grace

## Sitting with the Dying Sun

✦

## Poetic Interiors

52 Poems Presented in Seven Sectors

Gratitude in Grace ... xv
The Vision ... 21

1) Entering the Womb ... 31
2) Divine Mother at the Gate ... 41
3) Birth of the Sacred Heart ... 55
4) Ladies of Liberation! ... 63
5) Inn of the Ten Churches ... 77
6) Mystical Musings ... 87
7) Sitting with the Dying Sun ... 103

Dedication of Merit ... 119
Glossary ... 123
About the Author ... 132

# ✪ *Gratitude in Grace*

To Re-Emergence of the
Sacred Feminine

*H*eartfelt blessings to all entering here. Thank you for reading this collection of poems, which sprang from the depths of my heart like a thousand full moons of glowing light.

Gratitude in grace to all poets that inspire my day-to-day musings for the sake of sentient beings: Rendering your spirit on paper is no easy task.

Bless Jonathan, heroic best friend and husband of thirty-plus blissful years. Without his unwavering love, support and Soulful ear, this creative work—in present form—would not be possible. I love you eternally.

For gifting his delicious poem, *Mother* (you'll find on page 47) deep bows of praise and heartfelt blessings to a fierce luminary and life-mentor, the one-and-only Raja Yoga Master, philosopher Chandra Shekhar. He is a beloved Soul-friend to humanity. Our precious phone conversations continue to be an inspiring highlight to my day-to-day experiences. Dear reader, please hear his potent cry for transfiguration in the collective womb-space of the Sacred Feminine!

*Thug-je-che* (which means, thank you, in Tibetan) a thousand times to my heart-friend and spiritual father now residing beyond the sandy shores of samsara: His Eminence, the great Tibetan Nyingma-pa and Dzogchen Master, Venerable Khenchen Palden Sherab Rinpoche. Khenchen would have appreciated this poetic gathering rooted in joyful effort. His gentle voice in broken English mingles through this mutual mind-sphere, *"Na-cy, dees is wonderful."* May he return swiftly to Earth for the sake of all Creation.

To comrades on this sacred journey, like Dr. Joan Kaye, you offer a merry hand...making it all worthwhile.

For students, mentors, teachers, allies and SSFs (Soul-Sister-Friends) of The Three Times: past, present and future, I pay homage.

In particular, I wish to thank longtime esteemed colleague, SSF and partner in divine mischief, Reverend Dr. Linda Marie Nelson, who offered helpful comments to the introductory text when visiting our home in New Mexico. In the spirit of collaborative *Via Creativa*, upon hearing me read the poem entitled Ladies of Liberation! (see page 66) she swiftly delivered it a loving home at: www.shekinahruha.org. As I am now blessed beyond measure to be a member of this Mystical Community of The Sacred Feminine in the Order of Shekinah Ruha (OSR), I thank her as dear Abbess and co-founder. She had a vision with courage; and then "walked her talk" by taking sacred action to birth OSR.

An ocean of appreciation is in divine order to New York City-based Art Director extraordinaire, my dear lifelong friend Dawn Sebti. She designed a stunningly beautiful cover. As in my first book, *Doing a 360,* once again (without hesitation) she stepped forward to help illuminate heart-essence writings flowing through Soul. Our enduring bond is a true blessing.

I bend in amazing grace to many Soul-friends of the Multi-verse that decreed this collection with astonishing speed: simply put...they fancied it in your hands *asap*! From concept, writing, editing and publishing, *Garland of Grace* has been calm, unruffled and steady.

Therefore, traditional offerings of orange marigold garlands are given to an Ascended Master, HH Swami Śīvananda, who guides daily in bliss divine. I honor The Master as he continues to establish Light Platforms through humble Souls like me—called to do sacred work in their respective areas. And, here in the land of enchantment I pay tribute in soothing genuflection to a cherished Ancient One, Spirit-Mother of "The Anasazi."

Both these teachers are life-chaperons conspiring from beyond a diminishing veil to orchestrate projects such as this. You may glean from the glossary (which helps clarify and elucidate mystical terms used in some poems) that these revered torchbearers (one as Divine Father energy and the other as Sacred Feminine energy) beckon us from a verdant valley of *The Dreamtime*, while costumed in many holy forms. As a devoted Golden Daughter I kneel at their lotus feet while the Divine Feminine re-emerges in us all. Lha Gyalo!

With Love and Gratitude in Grace,
Nancy Ash
From the Land of Enchantment, New Mexico
Solar Eclipse of November 3, 2013

# ✸ The Vision

This humble collection of poetry was sparked from my courageous first poem, written at age eight. During that time-period a young female substitute teacher (in her twenties) told our class to draw with pencils and crayons to pass time. Instead, I was compelled to compose. It was divine revelry or what I call "Soul-Talk"—that's clear now. I'll never forget her kind encouragement—Soul-to-Soul—as she held open the black composition book, looked straight into my big baby blues and declared in certain revelation: "Ah...you can write! This is *very* good; please keep writing."

Words are powerful. Almost fifty years later I still feel the sacred stir of Soul in God's grace. Please allow *any* other name to arise in this moment for you as Divine: i.e., Presence, Source, Allah, Goddess, Jesus, The Tao, Christ Consciousness, Universal Mind, Buddha, Great Spirit or Oneness, etc. It is my life work in service to help midwife a glorious awakening and full flowering of Soul's conscious awareness in the heroic journey that we call, life. And I know that for some readers the word "God" may prompt a bit of unease and distance. Perhaps we may one day come to a contented time when it's "cool" to use it ubiquitously; like the popular acronym "OMG" written in texting—could "Oh My God!" be a heartening sign? I hope so...

Through the years, a fierce love of dharma *and* re-emergence of the Sacred Feminine in my daily studies, meditations, contemplations and prayers for all sentient beings stoked the fire to birth this nourishing assemblage you hold in your hands. As a devoted Tibetan Buddhist practitioner of the Vajrayana Dzogchen for many, many Moons, I've developed a profound kinship for the dharma, which are timeless teachings of The Buddha. Though I find boundless passion and comfort in *all* spiritual traditions, the path of dharma feels closest to non-dual heart, or, to my Soul.

Core to the dharma is a fundamental belief in the impermanence of all phenomena. I subscribe to this belief. All will pass away. All things must end. I won't be around two hundred years from now. And you won't, either. (Well, not in *this* body.)

Our Earth, sweet Gaia, will cease to provide safe refuge for her flock in about six billion years as a relatively low mass star (our Sun) finally starts to run out of hydrogen as fuel... and begins to burn out. I'm not a gloomy, morose poet. These are the inexorable facts of impermanence. So, the Sun is definitely dying. Not today or tomorrow, but one day in the far, far future the Sun will die. It's just true. It is as it is. And like the Sun, the moment you and I were born we were destined to die from this embodiment. As old yogi-friend Neela whispered with his scheming smile each year on my birthday, "You're one day closer to death!" It may sound weird, but I "got" that.

Dear reader, perhaps you may choose to sit next to me on a boundless cosmic bench with this seasoned and sobering practical knowing. As brilliant, world-renowned philosopher and Integral Evolutionary Theorist Ken Wilber says, "It's time for us all to 'wake up and grow up.'" When it comes to enlightenment...he has raised the bar. With a group of cherished colleagues from Humanitysteam.org, in 2013 I was blessed to visit with this astonishing luminary at his penthouse apartment in Denver on a sunny afternoon in May. As I reflect on this extraordinary day, realizations unfold a rare and benevolent gift of grace. Ken asked us to introduce ourselves, sharing our role and responsibilities in this global nonprofit organization I've worked for since 2011, as a member of the global council on a leading core team. Then he spoke tenderly about a dire need for the distinct and essential two processes for liberation: A developmental path of "growing up" is just as important as the traditional "waking up" meditative path to self-realization. From a kaleidoscopic lens of spiritual evolution, all traditions have these two different key dimensions. And like the Divine Masculine principle and re-emerging Sacred Feminine, both are inextricably bound.

As we all awaken to deeper levels of consciousness we must also mature in the structures of our spiritual development. Paraphrasing what Ken has said, "waking up to Emptiness or Oneness is not enough." We've got to grow up (mature emotionally), clean up our act (engage in consistent shadow-work) and most importantly "show up" embodied in an integral way. For me in this regard, I've needed many, many garlands of grace—a lot of practice, courage and fearless heart. I've realized the significance for my book's title. And, even if only one poem speaks to you—in a small measure, we too, are intricately connected.

Scientists speculate that a complete death of the Sun will take around a trillion years! No longer generating solar fusion, it will very slowly cool down to absolute zero. One theory declares it will begin to turn white-hot with temperatures boiling our oceans. Then the Sun will enter a red giant phase eventually ending its bright lifespan into a stellar black hole. Wow—that's mind-boggling, huh? What a nostalgic, provocatively mature interstellar contemplation and meditation *that* colossal process is. It is what it is.

In eastern sacred traditions, to practice meditation is commonly termed: to "sit" on the cushion. (Of course sitting on a chair counts as well.) So, we sit. We meditate and chant; we pray and contemplate; we study; and, we sit some more...every day, in every way. We just sit—that's it. Raising vibratory frequency with it, a compassionate non-dual understanding of non-clinging, non-attachment and non-grasping helps me make my way through this crazy, chaotic but fantastic world. Throughout many years of practice I've felt the call to serve. Initial Soul-pull came at age twenty when I entered the seminary in an interfaith metaphysical ministry. Ordination in 1985 followed six years of intense study, training and application in the healing arts. As a self-inquiring initiate coming full-circle, I've used and shared meditation, i.e., the "sitting" as a cornerstone to sacred practice communing with God.

Some mistakenly think that as a "reverend" then I must be Christian. I discover that a lot in most circles. In my sphere of influence some folks may be perplexed by titles and, who can blame them? It may be downright confusing. Titles, names, degrees, awards, celebrity, fame and such are just alluring trappings of postmodern life. Honestly, to wax poetic most days I'd rather be in a cave—in an octopus's garden...in the shade. I'm a simple mystic of the ancient ways. To say I am Buddhist or Christian or a Yogini or any other label like "poet" for that matter, wouldn't be further from the truth (well, my truth). I am integral, all encompassing and all-inclusive; I am the face of "I AM" before I was born. I am the mind of Big Mind. I am everything and no-thing. I am and, I AM. My current, long-term trans-denominational ministry serves all of Creation: Atheists, Agnostics, the God-loving and all creatures.

Like each precious bead of a rosary or mala—one-by-one—this garland of poems may assist our devotion as God's grace. In the least, these divine musings may yield delicious morsels of peace. The subtitle, *Sitting with the Dying Sun* is a metaphor for the inevitable death (like the aforementioned Sun) of an imbalanced Patriarchy, which has dominated our fractured world for way too long— thousands of years. In almost all cultures and spiritual traditions our life-giving hot Sun is a ubiquitous symbol or emblem for life's masculine principle. And our code of the feminine principle is commonly figurative in a milky-white, luminous Moon that glows in her fullness each month.

I'd like to get the following vital perspective clear out of the gate: Men aren't being bashed in this vision—far from it! But like our beloved father Sun, Patriarchy is dying too. The difference is that the fiery Sun shines bright while the ruling imbalanced Patriarchal Kingdom is in its very final stage of death, right now. Consider that this viewpoint is important. It's shared as a poetic trait of postmodern "waking up and growing up" integral philosophy. And holographically, the re-calibrated masculine aspect or "the Divine Masculine principle" *in union* with a rising "Divine Feminine principle" (in balance) is the only way that we, as a species, will survive for generations to come.

Let's look at it this way: A simple mathematical approach to seeing this mythology is: $1 + 1 = 3$, i.e., one (the Divine Masculine) plus one (the Sacred Feminine) equals *more* than two. I have sincere hearted trust that this current surfacing wave of consciousness (as a yoga, i.e., a fusion, marriage or union) will birth something unprecedented, transformative and potent—a vision quite spirited to a re-calibrated and therefore, renewed Earth. Yet, an emergence of the Divine Matriarchy (or Matrilineality, meaning that property is passed down through the maternal line on the death of the mother, not that of the father) won't be a historical re-do. Sister Crone and Old Hag wear fresh garments. The Maiden, Mother and Maga have a new and growing army of conscious women *and* men. The Sacred Feminine will not suppress her key creative nurturance under a stronghold of masculine energy any more. But a crucial awareness is that women must not suppress or dominate *each other* with their re-discovered power. *That* would be a sad abuse of tremendous gifts re-emerging. Let's face it; sons are born from the womb. Women create men from their mothering guidance. And women are born from that same womb! They must nurture women, too.

An integral rise of The Sacred Feminine is not about "women's lib"—it's liberation for everyone. We are all "growing up" together in this divine movement. A global healing augmentation will arise from the wretched dust of our collective misery into a fresh and wholesome gestalt—it must. Nature never repeats Herself, exactly. Our lives will weave an evolutionary tapestry of balance, i.e., Divine Mother *and* Divine Father (1 + 1 = 3).

This is my second book, an artistic departure from *Doing a 360: Turning Your Life Around to Follow Soul's Purpose*, an in-depth nonfiction guide to heroic spherical wholeness. As written in that work, "being is the ground for the doing." If not familiar with my "full-circle" teaching process as a spiritual mentor advocating Oneness, then I'm delighted you discovered this poetic garland. *Doing a 360* offers stories with "if I can do it, you can too" philosophy presenting strategies and exercises to inspire radical change from the Soul-level through a daily 360 Practice. The poetry you'll read in *these* pages dives deeper in an imaginative way, each a blessed medicine and creative companion to the collective yearning for: 1 + 1 = 3. Your contemplations of these poems in quiet moments of reflection (arising in a fortified, invigorated and inspired visionary mind-space) will help heal the current fragmented consciousness of humanity. To say that again simply: What you focus on becomes reality. And *your* vibration affects life. You may feel guided to read these poems with a loved one, sharing in sacred space by a golden fire or under the pleasant shade of a tree. So, welcome my friend. Sister or brother, come a little closer now. Grow comfortable in Soul-Talk. All are long awaited to feast at this table: Musings to celebrate the Re-emerging Sacred Feminine in harmony with the Divine Masculine. Herein, I sit naked "waking up and growing up" baring a holy heart-of-hearts—my Soul. It is an honor for you to read poems in *Garland of Grace: Sitting with the Dying Sun*. Chew and digest them slowly. Savor the sacred heart that beats in you and me. For in this moment, we *are* one.

As you sit
And read,
May these humble musings
Stir your heart...

May this garland of grace
Bless you
Whole.

✪

Note: The symbol ✪ indicates that a poem has ended. For your consideration, a glossary has been included to explain, as simply as possible, a few mystical words or terms used in this collection.

# ✸ Entering the Womb

## Spirit of the Womb

Spirit of the womb
Arises again:
She dwells among us
In drum and bell
She abides with all
In song and prayer.

Milk of the breast
Arises again:
She mingles
Through forests
She floats on seas.

Manna of the heart
Arises again:
She sermons
On paper pulpits
She dances
Beside rock, large and round.

Soul of Sacred Feminine
Arises again:
She loves
Each moment in joy and ease

She gives life
To The Oneness of All.

✤

## Womb of The Daughters and Sons

Tired and of thirst
I finally reached Turquoise Mountain
The crest, white with snow.
You were there, Brother, crying in the wind
Tears carried, like misty feathers...
Floating to Mother's hand.
Her golden stallion ready, silver-winged
Bent to ease a graceful mount.

She came forth
To this citadel of becoming
And tenderly, as handmaiden with honey and milk
Her elegant scarf caressed wet eyes, clenched
Wiping darkness away.
Then Divine Mother spoke
As ice melted around her robe:

"Daughters and Sons
That sleep in a bed of tears
Awaken! from tedious slumber of this tide
From this Great Dream
Know your bedchamber, dry."

✿

## Lone Wolf, Gone

Howling Wolf
On a bed of snow
Long season
Of Winter's discontent.

Pack scent
As talisman
Tipping few,
Hear the cry.

All gather
Feasting
On carrion of men.
Time of the lone Wolf,
Gone.

✪

## Octopus Medicine

Sweet Lady of the pool
Black hole
And friend of caves,
The charnel grounds await.

Mistress of all things
Appointment with an abyss
She rests,
Bolstered by rock and glass.

Temptress in disguise
Fluid limbs
Entwine prey in a prayer.

Goddess of The Three Times
She fades
To flowering dust and mud.

Mother
Of a changing tide,
I feed at your heart.

✪

## Octopus Medicine Re-visited

She squeezes through unfettered
Between cragging rocks of coral stone.
Ghostly apparition of The Three Times
She floats,
Undetected in charnel ground.

Soft, strategic gestures embrace
An ocean's lolling gaze
In Oneness dance.

She merges with all
In disguise
Colors blend with breath
In each moment.

Magical display of wisdom
She rests in-waiting for bards,
They hear her call.

Sacred sweet cave harbors her fluid,
A suppleness of becoming,
Enter this womb
As the Bardo of Being.

She mingles mind to The Ten Directions
And dies
A noble death to immortality.

✪

## Clarion Call of The Sacred Feminine

Shofar was blown
Piercing morning light of Father Sky —
Such resounding revelry!

Spiraling ram's horn
Woke the divine winds of change
To rising mud of Mother Earth.

An army of maidens
Rode in from the North, East, South and West.

Legions of Red Foxes and Ravens
Heard our cry!
Grouse danced her circle;
White Buffalo came in prayer.

Conch shell
Was lifted to The Ten Directions,
A bulbous vessel summoned Dakinis and men.

Drums beat as praise
To the heart of All gathered here.

✵

# Divine Mother at the Gate

## Divine Mother Tara

Divine Mother of The Three Times,
Bestower of compassion,
In 21-Ways
I know you.

You drink
My salty tears
Born of one,
Yourself.

Noble Lady
You caress my hair
To soothe
A troubled heart.

Sacred Feminine,
Spirit of the Dharma,
Eternal One, Tara
I feed at your breast.

✵

# Divine Mother at the Gate

I've dreamed you a thousand times
In many forms

I've played with your children
In every game

I've seen you in crowds
Before your time

I've heard your whispers
In the wind

I've tasted your nectar
In a flowing stream

I've felt your power
In the mountain thunderclap

I've dreamed you a thousand times
In many forms

Here with you I dwell,
Divine Mother.

✪

## Mother of The Cliff Dwellers

Anasazi Mother
I have not
Forgotten you.

Anasazi Spirit
I have not
Forsaken you.

Anasazi One
I run
To you.

Lady of the Ancient Ones
I hear
Your call.

Mother of The Cliff Dwellers
I sit
With you.

Sacred Feminine of my heart
We beat
As one.

✪

## Loving Each Other, Again

I saw Mary and Tara
Dancing on clouds
Holding hands to the Sun.

I saw Machig Labdrön and Ma'at
Spinning gold threads
Chanting hymns to the Goddess.

I saw Grandmother and Gaia
Sipping tea by the Moon
To The Ten Directions.

I saw you and me
Bowing to each other
Singing praise in prayer.

I saw women and men
Balanced between mirrors
Loving each other, again.

✪

## Mother by Chandra Shekhar

There's nothing that can compare
To the wonder, grandeur or magnificence
Of a mature
Psychologically healthy
Spiritually inclined female.
She is one without a second.
The mother of all.
The greatest creature in all of creation.
The most brilliant idea ever conceived.

✻

## Mystic's Heart

From inside
Access the unitive heart.
In Christ's breath
Merge with Mother's myth.

Release adhesiveness
Embrace the flow

From the core
Open this Creator's heart.
In Brigit's dance
Blend with Ma'at's song.

Burn the mask
Enfold the world

From the well
Enter a mystic's heart.
In Tao's whisper
Mingle with Buddha's tale.

Pardon sludge
Kiss the Sun

✸

# Full Moon on Chaco Canyon

Anasazi Mother, by light of Blue Moon I see and write
Pre-dawn musings in August sphere:
You awakened me this hour to dance, as *da capo*
Toes sink in ancient sand
Pottery shards beckon sages
Like calling cards of destiny…
Each story in grey line and squiggle
From clay dais of ancestral winds.
Ancient Ones gather at the gallows of Chaco:
Women and men enraptured by swinging demons
Of hatred, greed, unknowing and rust.
Ornamental omens measured in marveled gaze,
Boundless as shunyata
Ancient Mother snatches us from jaws of death
In this chimera of "no-dream"
Dogma-smashers congregate to bind the masses
As a green labyrinth of endless dahoons.
Tribes of Elders arrive in truth-tone echoes
Through rock and hill

A daleth opens again for those who see
Shadows, transparent at canyon's edge.
Bustling authority assembles at Wrath's Trial
As celestial hosts declare dominion on despair,
This long, cold night.
Obscurations leap, tremble and flutter, no more.
Primal Mother, radiance fills this brick-room
In resplendent Moonbeams
Luster and glint as residue streaming
Enfranchise, as Angels' wings.
Walls are held by sky as a ceiling ascends
To The Tsar of Becoming.
108 courtiers wait at the bath
As ignorance, with her blind-spot
Rests on your fawning couch no more.
Welcome, elixir! — She visits by light of the Moon
Replenished in her fullness
Rotund in venerated hand,
Divine Mother lures from slumber
All who wait at the window...
For triumphant return.

✪

## Mary at the Gate

Mary at the cross
I weep for you.

Mary at the tomb
I cry for you.

Mary at the gate
We meet for the first time.
In exultation
You take my hand.

Mary at the Passover meal
I eat with you.

Mary at the graveyard
I dance with you.

Mary at the mountain
We melt into one.
In joy
I take your robe.

✪

# ✸ Birth of the Sacred Heart

## Birth of the Sacred Heart

Today I was born
Slapped in the face for the first time.

ALL was fresh
ALL was new
Until the next birth...

And then I was born again, and again.
ALL was clear
ALL was calm
Until the next birth...

And then I was born again, and again.
ALL was pure
ALL was true
Until the next birth...

And then I was born again, and again.
Today I was born, again.

✪

## Postpartum Blues

Solstice has come and gone
Postpartum blues,
But has the Sun been missed in cloud?

New World birth has come and gone
Not much arose in chariot's fire,
But has the Moon been missed in cloud?

Calendar has come and gone
No end in sight,
But has the sky been missed in cloud?

Soul has come and gone
In this moment so fresh,
But have the stars been missed in cloud?

✪

## Buddha Nature

Today I woke up, again.
My friends, the sky and bowing limbs
Mourned my passing
In delight.

Today I woke up, again.
The air, so clean
Coaxed leaves to dance, unfettered
In wind.

Today I woke up, again.
To thoughts, inquired at their base
And quaking
In crumbling foundation.

Today I woke up, yet again.
This moment, so free and alive to the everything
And nothing
In Grace.

✿

## Midwife to The Birth

Last night peace came to the world
I undressed to the bone
While Alchemy's daughters and sons flew in.

Twelve Ravens, half red-mother and half father-white
Entwined as celestial flesh.
Twelve strands of liquid mind, resting in fresh DNA
Calmed an elixir of the 10,000 fermenting things.

A Snowy Owl sat on my knee
And fed from new hands
While six Mother Ravens laid their Spring eggs
In the marrow of sacred heart.

Last night peace came to the world
I licked the sugary batter bowl dry
As Maya's party left the scene.

✪

## Pilgrimage of the Sacred Heart

She whispered from sacred heart
A desert wasteland hung
As clouds covering sky.
Mounds of promise in each puffy hill
Crouched by a Blue Moon.
Crossing this desert wilderness was light
Torches carried on high
By Sky Walkers of The Three Times.
The Divine Feminine
Trekked across starlit sands above.
Soul's journey vast in this awakening,
Crystal camels came
Adorned in turquoise saddles
Holding fields of grain.
Pilgrimage of the Sacred Heart:
Beloved Mother, forever to you I run
Oasis on clouds
Quenches thirst.

✸

# Light on Flower

Grateful for communion —
Light on flower
Resting in Divine Father
Lying down with Sacred Mother.
They nurse in truth
As we hold hands for the New Birth.

✪

# ✴ Ladies of Liberation!

## Sisterhood, Brotherhood

Sister, I hold you
Friend not foe.
Brother, I hold you
Gratitude in grace.

Sisterhood, we call you
Gate open for all to pass.
Brotherhood, we call you
Arms wide, enfold the day.

Helping hands reach
Wound in blood
Feasting relieves, hunger and thirst.

Communion calls
A fiery torch sprays flame to dust.
Longing grows, until burst to tears —
Love deepens.

Sacred Feminine, I kiss you
Crone without fear.
Divine Masculine, I embrace you
Gift of God.

✺

## Ladies of Liberation!

Ladies of Liberation!
Your time has come, again.
Arise unfettered this morning.

Lift your chalice and sip
Alone, together at this well.

Vestments of rainbow-light robes
As fruit, savored and shared.

Divine Mother returns
Like flowers of the field.

Each fragrance a perfume,
A thousand bursting-hearts delight.

Each prayer on melted knee
Enfolds as tattered shawls
Ancient devotion cloaked in warmth.

Ladies of Liberation!
Your time has come, again.
Arise unfettered this morning.

Breathe her spirit, Shekinah Ruha
Into this dark night.

Ladies in-waiting!
Your time has come, again.
Raise vibrant lamps to an indigo sky.

Ladies of The Three Times!
The gate is open.

We, as a pool of pearls bathe away dust.
Milky-white, our heart-essence runs
Like rivers from One Source.

Ladies of Liberation!
Your time has come, again.
Arise unfettered this morning.

Welcome.

✸

## Dawn of The Fae

Today I met a girl
Of fairy, of Fae
I knew her before,
Before this day.

Our eyes met
In kaleidoscopic view
Her shimmering coat, new.

Today I met a girl
Of fairy, of Fae
I knew her before,
Before this day.

Our hearts melted
In mystical song
Her humming voice, dawn.

✪

# The Way of Chöd

Today I sat with pity
And, kicked her out to the curb

Lying there... bleeding
She begged for a kind hand

With back turned in scorn,
A legion of Skywalkers appeared at the door
Bearing gifts of flowers
And scented oils

We fed the hungry ghost
Who came no more

✵

# Return of Black Lilith

Black Lilith was there at gilded door.
She knocked three times...
Shekinah, as All Sabbath Queens
Welcomed her in.

Gifts of drink and feasting plate:
Fig and pomegranate,
Rare teas, partnered with tartlets of One-Taste;
Pillows for black crown and anointed feet
Poised soft and golden in thread of the lamb.

We encircled in loving embrace.
Ears leaned-in, tilted and bowed for every Psalm
She revealed tales of a long voyage:
Finding her way through Moonlight, black
From dark dungeons
From bleak underworlds
From blighted days.

Black Lilith spoke of her rise from lower realms:
The Root,
The Second Secret Space
And the Dark Sun

Then she sang softly with Tingsha and Drum:
Her ascension
Her re-emergence
Her ride up to *this* house.
Black Mother shed tears in relief
As young men
Gazing through windows in hot breath on the glass,
Begged to enter.

One-by-One
They rang the bell at our door.
Wedding complete in red and white wine
Gushing from a boundless cup of evolution.
Fifth man blew a beloved shofar
While the Sixth and Seventh
Bent their knees in prayer,
Like Foo Lions guarding the nest.
All merged in sacred heart.

Pachamama drank from this Cosmic Well:
Healing her whole... as rivers sparkled clean
As oceans stirred renewed
As fracking wounds closed
As toxins dissolved in apple and bone
As cancer sores melted
As forests returned to the land
As we smelled lush grass, again.

Men came down
Black Lilith and her sister friends, flew up.
The 4th Green Seal had been opened:
All poured in
Never to look back.

✪

## Liberation

Licking salty wounds,
I drink the nectar
Of good
And bad.

I taste tears,
Of in
And out.

Impoverished heart
Yields to pregnant grace.

Birth rips naked
To fresh blood,
In liberation.

✪

## Garland of Grace

Sisters of Oneness, I weep at your feet
Scattered to corners as dust from the broom.
Space between us feels vast in Maya's wily embrace.
A raging fire burns from the heart
As Gabriel stands above in sweet bugle horn.
This wretched longing eats soft flesh as demon-child,
Sucking dry the crystal temple of becoming.
Shawls enfold, wiping tears from a silken eye
Raining this fresh dawn.
Open arms engulf voyaging wombs as
Sobbing tales spark the life, anew.

Friends of Oneness, sadness grips as steel-flower
Waiting for harvest fruit of vintage vine.
Time between us feels prolonged as jester's silly coat.
A rankled sore oozes from Soul's gate
As Dakinis dance on starlit clouds.
This wretched longing knocks at my door as demon-child,
Its scythe slicing fledgling grain of promised field.
Whispers mingle in silent white hue
Calling the New Earth.
Broad smiles caress our Sacred Feminine while
Endearing hands hold tight.

Ladies of Oneness, I kneel at your robes
Rainbow threads weave the dress.
Emptiness between us feels deep in Coyote's trick.
Dizziness from waning veil dulls my mind
As Durga stomps her lotus feet.
This wretched longing tears the cloth as demon-child,
Blocking light as lovers apart in their wish-fulfilling jewel.
Heartache comes as bold thieves
In rays of the Sun.
Anointing oils and perfume appear
To mask the deed.

Sisters of Oneness, burden lives no more
Noble death to thousands who grieve.
Separation between us bears false witness
In this garland of grace.
A tender joy eats our sorrows
As Miriam sips from the well.
This wretched longing comes no more as demon-child,
Our begging bowl full in liquid gold.
Courage reigns as Queen and King
Timeless ocean of seasonal tide.
Yearning a presence of The Beloved in our vows
We remain entwined and kiss eternity.

✿

# ✸ *Inn of the*

# *Ten Churches*

## The One-Taste

The feast before us of rainbow-light:
Fruits of color and taste, divine.
Next to me
Goddess in white.

The feast before us of flowing field:
Each plate of season and luscious bowl.
Across from me
Goddess in black.

The feast before us of manna and wine:
Cups of prayer and peace, delight.
Round table
All shades of the womb.

The feast before us of sweetened cake:
Each bite of nectar, the One-Taste.
In my chair
Sister came to greet.

✪

## Dine with Demons

Dine with demons…
Feed them well.

Tempt with obscurations at the table.
Feast with your devil, she hungers no more.
Scrolling gossip of mind, arise in non-grasping
Satiated by your generous hand.
Tangible demon of *this* world and of *that,*
Drink with us; raise your glass to The Ten Directions.

Outer enemy of magical display
Empty your bowl 108 times.
Inner devils at the core
Please dine with boundless delight.
Devour dear demons, all I have cooked.
Savor my being — each bone, all flesh.

Dine with demons…
Feed them well.
Offer your heart on a plate
As the One-Taste.

✪

## Inn of the Ten Churches

Today I entered the Ten Churches:

The sky hovered
The winds blew
The clouds sang
The ground sat
The rain poured
The trees folded
The rocks praised
The ants mingled
The flowers exalted
My heart bowed.

✪

## Feast of the Great Union

Gabriel's horn in clarion call
Summons, daughters and sons.
Hearts burst to deafening blow
As heaven's gate opens — mile-high.

Tara's compassion of rainbow-light
Beckons, daughters and sons.
Minds' flowering in emptiness fields
As salvation's portal, bares eons — deep.

Great Spirit's knowing as light of the Sun
Harkens, daughters and sons.
Souls flock to her Earth-cry
As enlightenment's bloom this moment — is.

Kali's power at edge of night
Warns, daughters and sons.
Temples gather to hold hands
As God's grace abides — eternal.

Tao's nothingness in ease, a simple way
Invites, daughters and sons.
Joy from freedom of thoughts' chain
As Being's ground unfolds — holy.

✦

## Land of the Temples

Land Ho!
Sacred ground like old world travelers
We rest.

Land Ho!
Break ground to ten thousand temples
We rest.

Land Ho!
Holy ground to new lights ablaze
We rest.

Land Ho!
Groundless ground to water again
We rest.

Land Ho!
No more
We are found.

✪

# Feast at the Inn of the Ten Churches

Today I feast in the garden.
The table set
In boundless cue.

Guests arrive on time.
Together and apart,
Dining at
The Inn of the Ten Churches.

✦

# ✺ Mystical Musings

## Blessed Be!

Praise be to the one that broke my heart.
Praise be to the one that snuffed out light.
Praise be to the one that kidnapped youth.
Praise be to the one that bargained with death.
Praise be to the one that blocked the door.
Praise be to the one that hacked soft flesh.
Praise be to the one that sprinkled salt in the wound.
Praise be to the one that fed my pen to the fire.
Praise be to the one that smashed clay to dust.
Praise be to the one that raped a muse.
Praise be to the one that stole pad and brush.
Praise be to the one that pushed me off the cliff.
Praise be to the one that soured green field.
Praise be to the one that closed the curtain.
Praise be to the one that sat on the red hat.
Praise be to the one that ransomed a Soul.
Praise be to the one that leaves me hungry.
Praise be to the one that comes no more.

✪

## Gratitude

Morning breaks —
A sweet symphony of delight,
Music to my ears

Distance roof hammers' blow
Unceasing
Thump, as the heart, beats

Car engines and sweeping brooms
Mingle
In jet planes above

Trashcans drag in soft inclines
To nesting places
Of square caves

A steel-saw, grind
Unforgiving
On wood in this morning peace

Gratitude unfolds and enfolds
In sound —
I can hear!

✪

## Nocturnal Bandit

Illness comes as a thief in the night.

She steals
Your stories into new ones — fresh, yet bitter.

She rips
The cloak from your tattered being.

She strips
You naked of all possessions.

She robs
You in sorrow, betrayal and fear.

She takes
From you, everything — to charnel ground
And buries the tale forever.

She comes
To take you home
Where you've never been before.

✪

## Losing The Lama

Upon knees and one hand
The other
Clutches my heart.

Bleeding bindu-drops
Soak the floor
In puddles of grief.

They merge
In silent weeping
With essence of cream.

Tears of The Three Times
Red and white,
Rigpa dissolves to shunyata.

Losing the Lama:
Love forever lives...

✪

## Relic of The Red Hat Lama

Red Hat
Fierce Lion
Master of Nine
The One

Teachings Exalt
Nyingma
3 Roots
3 Times

Dharma Dance
Hammer on Stone
Stainless Joy
Compassion, Inexorable

Father
Mother
Brother
Friend

Tender Hands
Sky Heart
Lotus Feet
Gone, Thus Gone

Dzogchen King
Buddha to All
Mingling Mind
Our Tears Rain

Bone Relic
Here,
There,
Everywhere...
Ahh...  Ahh...  Ahh...

*PHAT!*

✦

## Contemplations

Contemplation: Is the woman
She's battered,
Abused stepdaughter of nimble light.

Contemplation: Is the man
He's shackled,
Bound stepson in thought and deed.

Contemplations: Are the masses
They're neglected,
Lonely stepchildren at elegant hallways.

Contemplation: Is the friend
You've never wed,
Maid of honor to a thousand brides.

Contemplation: Is the companion
You're runner-up,
Again and again.

Contemplation: Is the One
I've found you at last,
Feast now at the head of my table.

✵

## Middle Ground

Breeze greets here
As knotty pine

Salamander safe
In revelry at my feet

Hummingbird close
Guards The View, in joy

Below or above
In worlds of Dreamtime

I rest a gaze between,
Middle Ground.

✦

### Radiant Beam

Of crackle,
In fiery dawn
They whisper.

In mire,
At drowning dusk
They whimper.

With shadow,
On demon night
They cry.

A glimmer,
To radiant beam
They rejoice.

✸

## Wisdom of the Hummingbird

Sweet bird of the hum
You pause
In me.

Tasting nectar
We giggle
And... fly on!

✪

## Three Good Friends

Winter, Sun and Wind
All good friends to me
Hurling us from darkness
Winter, with her brother Sun, befriends.
Warm, steady and strong; he hugs me close,
Radiant ray to dry tears.
Oh! Winter days, my friends, you heal a heart
There is peace in light.
Constant, caressing — singing her song
Through canyon and over the hill
Sister Wind cries in joy.
A true friend, she took blowing dust as a lover.
My good pals, these three
Winter, Sun and Wind
Sparkling chimes tingle as the poet's paper
Ruffles-up a fresh page.
Oh! Good friends have come to tea
Surround me in your One-Taste as nectar prose.
Stay with me tonight
Party in slumber as pillow-feathers glide!
Don't leave… or I shall die.
Yet, death is a must this day — I know that now.
It is the pill of salvation
An elixir of the roused
Die I must to the affections of lies and falsehood.

Down this well I must plunge
Reborn in Winter, Sun and Wind that befriend
So kind in cloak and hand.
My three dearest friends
You greet in this dark night of the Soul
Where demons dwell with foul drool.
Where evil boils its sour bones
Where fallen-ones beckon and tempt
Like those in dark alleys
With ghoulish eyes to pierce the black sky.
Oh! Good friends, Winter, Sun and Wind
Stay a little longer in our repose this day.
Grant a holiday of peace in the world through my eyes
Visit long and deep in warm breath.
Commune heartedly in these days remaining
Linger a little longer... dally here
For a need is great to bare this Soul.
You listen as a mother to her child
You hear the call in daughter's heart
You feel the longing, this day to never end.
But it does in death, down a cold valley, again
As great Snowy Owls emerge
Taking flight upon the last star
When friends return,
Clutching a scarf in gusts of morning, mountain air
When russet leaves blow-in upon my cheek.
All pause a fleeting moment in the Sun.

Three good friends I can count on,
They do not betray.
Winter-long offers time to rest
Wind's song stirs my Soul
Sun's light feeds each cell of this formless form.
How can I go wrong with friends like these?
They don't deceive
They do not lie.
Alone here, I am blessed
In peace with no thing needed
Thirst quenched
Hunger quelled.
Sitting with three good friends
Love grows like buried roots of Sister Spring.
Inexorable, unceasing, yet unborn
I ready myself for the next death tonight
When eyes close to all I have worn that day,
To all I've seen and said and done.
Tomorrow the Winter will still be here
Sun and Wind, good friends of the days to come.
Chaperones of Spirit, let me take your hand
Guide me — don't let go of your loving grip
Until the night ends and peace, remains.

✪

# ✸ Sitting with the Dying Sun

## Big Mind

Wisdom Traditions
Bouquet of rainbow flowers,
Like a bride I carry these at my breast.
Truth purveyors
Crowd of colored faces,
Like an usher I greet them all.

Sacred texts
Pile of paper and scroll,
Like a librarian I dowse the word.
Big Mind
Nondual circle of prayer,
Like a friend I sit with the light of a dying Sun.

✺

## I Sit Alone with You

I sit alone
With crowds of one,
I sit alone with you.

I sit alone
With thoughts of thousands,
I sit alone with you.

I sit alone
With universe so vast,
I sit alone with you.

I sit alone
With charnel ground,
I sit alone with you.

I sit alone
With clamoring residue and starch,
I sit alone with you.

I sit alone
With a dying Sun,
I sit alone with you.

I sit alone
With daggers and death,
I sit alone with you.

I sit alone
With every star and cloud,
I sit alone with you.

I sit alone
With all Souls,
I sit alone with you.

I sit alone
With each birdsong,
I sit alone with you.

I sit alone
With clarion call in joy,
I sit alone with you.

I sit alone
With it all,
I sit alone with you.

I sit alone
With God in rapture,
I sit alone with you.

I sit alone
With no one,
I sit alone with you.

✵

## Graveyard of Becoming

Today I wept
At the graveyard,
Nothing appeared
Except this moment
In you

Today I wept
At the graveyard,
Nobody came
Except the blood drinkers
In rapture

Today I wept
At the graveyard,
No one heard
Except the wind dancers
In glee

Today I wept
At the graveyard,
No one saw
Except this moment
In you

✸

## Mind

Grasping mind is the trouble
Clinging mind is the foe
Attached mind is the pain

Big Mind is the freedom
Open Mind is the friend
Relaxed Mind is the joy

Seamless Mind is the One-Taste
Vast Mind is the lover
Unnamable Mind, is

✪

## The Nondual One

10,000 thoughts arise in sitting…
Blessed be!
The dying Sun ablaze

Mind in heart springs Oneness…
Blessed be!
The waxing Moon glows

Heart in mind unites field…
Blessed be!
The Nondual personal in each voyage

Ropes release their grip to the wind…
Blessed be!
And boats sail on.

✪

## Monkey Mind

Peeling a banana
Teases monkey mind.

Tyranny of thought
Feeds wild boar.

Agenda in thinking
Offers grist for the mill.

Orbit of prayer
Plays the rise and fall.

Red string remembers
Clouds of unknowing.

Sitting with the dying Sun
Opens palm to heroic sweetness.

10,000 opportunities
Let go in a gesture of ease.

✸

## The Letting-Go

Thoughts ascend on gilded bench
Like hills approached
Steep incline effort, and then

The letting-go, the letting-go

Decent in ease offers mind's release
A letting-go, a letting-go
Up and down, over and over
Attentions arise like looming hills that never end

The letting-go, the letting-go

Walking up, mound's end is near in bliss
Trekking down, the bottom yields another knoll
Contemplations appear like hills managed
Up and down, immeasurable as the Sun's rays
Sitting still and
Letting-go, in the letting-go

✪

## The Winds of Oneness

In the wind
I hear God
As Goddess in grace

In a breeze
Songs of Enoch sprinkle as fresh rain.
Pages from Thomas,
A Gospel of Mary and James,
Each turn with gentle gust

In the roaming air
So longstanding and yet new,
Chimes nudge from exposed Psalms.
Dazzling solicitations soothe my Soul

In the wind
I hear Goddess
As God in grace

All that was hidden, found
In light of the dying Sun:
Mary's nine children, not eight
Yeshua's blackened young hand
Cain's wife, bare
Giants from Angels fallen into the womb.

In each whispering breath
Truth knocked at heart's door:
How would life ever be the same?
How could days end this night?
How will children heed the spiraling winds of change?

In this rustle of leaves
I know God
As Goddess in grace

In swaying branches that halt and dive
Divine Father has come for lunch
With his date,
Sacred Mother relishes a gilded sword upon his brow.
Blowing sands on rippled pond
Show the way to a jubilant wind.

Help us to see
Women and Men in prayer holding hands
Help us to know
Divine Masculine wed to his sacred girl
Help us to be
One, in compassionate fruit.

In billowing robes,
Which flutter as wings
We stand,
Arms out to the winds of Oneness.

In the airstream
I hear God
As Goddess in grace

Two sides of a luminous coin
From starry pockets they rest
On the velvet church-plate of love.

In the whirlwind
There is Oneness
As a garland of grace

✪

## Ablaze in the Dying Sun

Today my wait is over.
I bow before you, boundless Moon and Sun
I kneel at your lotus feet
A thousand have come
To hear you speak
As flowers bend in ease to your gaze

Today my wait is over.
I curtsy through folds of flowing robe
Offering diamonds in praise
A thousand have come
To see at this gate
While hearts tremble in glorious fervor

Today a long wait is over.
Today I am, with you.

✸

# ✵ Dedication of Merit

By the merit of this practice
I dedicate myself to all creation.

May all be awakened from heartbreak to bliss.
May all taste the treasure of ultimate seeing.
May all train their heart.
May all do kind deeds.
May all see the suchness.
May all feel grateful in this moment.
May all hear the clarion call.
May all enter the depths.
May all touch their lips in a divine kiss.
May all know certainty in the letting-go.
May all speak their truth.
May all drink from the red and white chalice.
May all be graced.
May all simply be, love.

May it be so. So be it.

✵

# ✿ Glossary

**108 times** refers to 108 counting beads strung on a mala, which is used for recitation of mantras in spiritual practice (known as japa in Sanskrit). In the eastern traditions like Hinduism, Buddhism, Jainism, as well as Raja Yoga, etc., 108 has sacred significance of varying degrees. In Sanskrit, the word mala means garland.

**Anasazi** is a Navajo word, a common term used by archaeologists for "the Ancient Ones" or ancient Puebloans (Pueblo People) of the Southwest USA. Many modern ancestors do not use the term, Anasazi. A more appropriate expression of honor is: The Ancient Ones. With great respect to our ancestors, I've used the word in these poems to draw attention to this delicate issue, rendered here briefly. Pueblo means "village" in Spanish, originating with explorers of this American region.

**Bardo** is a Tibetan word meaning, between or literally, intermediate or transitional. Bardo refers generally to a complex intermediate state of being or consciousness that is between human death and re-birth, i.e., the Bardo of Dying. It begins the moment consciousness leaves the body, and ceases the moment consciousness enters the body of the next life. Reincarnation is a core belief of Tibetan Buddhists, and accordingly there are six different Bardos or states. Death and dying is a common topic in Buddhist teachings with the traditional view that the Death Bardo lasts 49 days. Practitioners pray for the deceased during this rich time-period. Suggested reading: *The Great Liberation Through Hearing in the Bardo (The Tibetan Book of the Dead)* by Francesca Fremantle and Chögyam Trungpa.

**Bindu**, a Sanskrit term for drop, literally translates to "dot" or a "point." It's the source of creation or ultimate nectar. Bindu is a sacred energy aspect of the subtle body. There is a potent red and white bindu of the female and male, respectively manifest as menses blood and sperm.

**Black Lilith** is the powerfully alluring ancient female figure and archetype of primordial mystery, magic and truth whose origins are shrouded in timelessness. She has re-emerged astrologically (as a symbolic point) during this time-period as Black Moon Lilith, which is connected to our present Earth-Moon cosmological configuration. Rising from some smoky-like rumors, she abides with us now as a vibrant balancing factor to "goodness" and masculinity, asserting herself in a healing, mirror-like wisdom fury. Misconstrued perceptions of the dark Black Madonna or Black Mother as fearful, painful and of loss (rather than gain) have contributed to a gross misunderstanding of the regenerative beauty and power of Lilith. It has been said that man rules the day (our dying Sun), and the luminary of night is dominated by the Sacred Feminine—spirit of Black Moon Lilith. Dramatic and beguiling Dark Goddess Lilith teaches discernment and so, so much more! Like others (in this Glossary) such as Kali and Machig Labdrön, she helps us to cut through illusions if we are truly ready to "grow up" under her fierce, dark shadowed tutelage. The Queen of The Night Lilith appeared in literature around 2000 BCE as handmaiden to Sumerian Goddess, Inanna. In Hebrew myth she was the notorious first "wife" of Adam, and was exiled near the Red Sea as a tempest wind-spirit representing the female transpersonal shadow, i.e., "the bad girl." A neglected and banished Shekinah, powerful Lilith was consort to God himself. Explore her further in books: *Black Moon Lilith* by astrologer M. Kelley Hunter; and, *The Book of Lilith* by Jungian analyst, Barbara Black Koltuv, Ph.D.

**Brigit** or **Brigid** (the Exalted One) is Goddess of The Celtic, Pagan tradition and Irish mythology. Saint Brigit of Kildare, Ireland lived in the 6th Century. Her feast day is celebrated on February 1.

**Chaco Canyon** is one of the most powerful, revered and famous archaeological areas of the world, a sacred desert vortex of well preserved land-ruins in northwest New Mexico where the ancient Pueblo People lived between 850 and 1250 AD. Once a major center of spiritual living, ceremony and trade, Chaco Culture is a shallow, ten-mile canyon (70 miles from the nearest town). It's open to the public for pilgrimage functioning as a U.S. National Historic Park.

**Charnel ground** or cemetery is referred to often in ancient Tibetan texts as a place for practicing Chöd.

**Chimera** means fantasy.

**Chöd** is a Tibetan word meaning "cutting through" and is pronounced, Cho or Chuh (the "d" is silent). It is a sacred, powerful spiritual practice founded by the female Tibetan Saint, Machig Labdrön. Her intense sadhana (practice) was revitalized by the 21st Century American female Tibetan Lama, Tsultrim Allione. Please consider visiting Taramandala.com

**Coyote Medicine** is known as wisdom of "the Trickster" in certain Native American Spirituality tribes.

**Da capo** is an Italian musical term for starting over or "take it from the top."

**Dahoons** are evergreen hedges in the holly family.

**Dais** is a throne or a raised platform used for speaking or performing. Dais is pronounced, DAY-is.

**Dakinis**, pronounced "Dah-keen-ees" is Sanskrit for "Sky Walkers" or "Sky Dancers" referring to the potent Sacred Feminine aspect of enlightened beings. They are core to Tibetan Buddhist teachings. (The Tibetan word for Dakinis is Khandros.)

**Daleth** represents a sacred doorway. It is the fourth letter of the Hebrew alphabet.

**Dogma** means rules; fundamental religion has dogma.

**Durga** is an important Hindu Goddess that destroys evil-forces. The Mother Goddess, she represents the power of ALL the Gods combined. Durga means "invincible."

**Dzogchen** is a Tibetan term for the Great Perfection, the Great Completion, or the "utterly complete" path to liberation. In Sanskrit the word is, Atiyoga. Pronounced "zog-CHEN" the "d" is silent with emphasis on the second syllable. This awakened state of mirror-like wisdom is a central and pinnacle teaching of Tibetan Vajrayana Buddhism, recognizing our true or Buddha nature. Our true nature is of Emptiness or Oneness — ultimate, unfabricated and primordially pure. Dzogchen is a pinnacle path of immediate liberation through a complete understanding that all of life, "is as it is." (Consider Ken Wilber's integral theory of "waking up *and* growing up.")

**Fae** refers to legendary sacred beings called Fairies.

**Foo Lions** are Tibetan lion-like guard dog statues always used in pairs, i.e., female and male. They flank and protect any entrance with fierce flair. A slang term "dog" has been used in the West. Traditionally they're called Guardian Lions.

**Gabriel,** of the Abrahamic Religions, is a beloved and powerful Archangel of Revelation known for blowing his trumpet as a Divine Messenger. There are 32 Biblical verses about Gabriel, one of only two angels named in the Bible. Gabriel means "man of God" or "strength of God."

**Gaia** is the Greek Goddess of our Earth, and also the name for a modern scientific hypothesis (coined in 1970) by a UK chemist, James Lovelock. This cosmological concept is: Our planet is a single, self-regulating system or cell with a living and breathing consciousness connecting to all. Therefore, Gaia is an actual living-spirit or entity of our planet, i.e., Mother Earth. The word Gaia is pronounced, GUY-ah.

**Gestalt** is a German word meaning shape, configuration or form. Here in this book, *Garland of Grace*, it refers to the English "holistic" concept of wholeness in Gestalt psychology, i.e., the whole is greater than the sum of its parts (1+1 = 3).

**Kali** is an awesome and powerful Hindu Goddess known as the Black or Dark Mother that destroys! Goddess Kali is quite ferocious as a Mother protecting her child.
   *"My child, you need not know much in order to please Me. Only Love Me dearly. Speak to me, as you would talk to your mother, if she had taken you in her arms." - Unknown*

**Labyrinth** is not a maze. You cannot get lost on your sacred journey walking through a circular labyrinth. Where you enter...you also exit. It is a single path or unicursal tool for spiritual transformation, a lovely ancient practice revitalized in recent decades. (Please see Chapter 3: The Sacred Circle from my book, *Doing a 360: Turning Your Life Around to Follow Soul's Purpose*.) Also visit the labyrinthsociety.org

**Lama** is a Tibetan word for a title of chief, teacher or Guru. Guru is Sanskrit, meaning teacher, master or "one who removes the darkness."

**Lha Gyalo!** is a Tibetan phrase (pronounced, la-jahl-low); an exuberant expression of joyful victory to the deities. During ceremonious end of Dzogchen retreats my teacher, Venerable Khenchen Palden Sherab Rinpoche would gather us in a circle, jump up in the air and shout: "Lha Gyalo!"

**Ma'at** is the supreme African/Egyptian Goddess of Truth.

**Machig Labdrön**, (Unique Mother Torch of Lab) lived in Tibet from 1055 – 1149 AD. She is the only Tibetan Buddhist woman-founder of a practice lineage, which is called Chöd. And as such, Machig is a renowned Tibetan tantric practitioner and revered teacher often depicted as a Dakini, or enlightened female energy. She used a large damaru (drum) and a bell during the powerful practice (sadhana) of Chöd (the "cutting-off" ritual). She said, "As long as there is an ego, there are demons."

**Maga** is an Italian word meaning, enchantress, witch or feminine magician. Maga is a contemporary term used in Sacred Feminine circles to represent the seasoned yet fruitful stage of life known as "The Queen." Magi (plural of magus) is a term used since 6th century BC to denote followers of Zoroaster. In the Christian traditions (Gospel of Matthew) the Magi (wise men from the east) followed a Star of Bethlehem and thus visited the infant Jesus.

**Manna** is Hebrew for sacred food from heaven (according to the Bible). It's usually bread, yet not exclusively. Manna is a miraculous, general spiritual nourishment of divine origin. The word also appears in the Qur'an.

**Mary** in these poems refers to our sacred Mother Mary, mother of Jesus or Yeshua; and also Mary Magdalene, who is re-emerging in her rightful place as the Mother of the Divine Feminine. Consider reading *The Magdalene Path* by Claire Sierra.

**Maya** means illusion (or delusion) in Sanskrit. It is an important mystic term in Vedanta, Sikhism, Hinduism and Buddhism, etc.

**Miriam** is a Jewish name for the woman that did good deeds for her people. Sister of Moses, she is a beloved embodiment of the Sacred Feminine (Miriam's Cup or Well).

**New World** refers here in *Garland of Grace* to the post-Mayan calendar ending date of December 21, 2012. Obviously, the world didn't "end." Perhaps the way we "knew it" did end...?

**Octopus Medicine** is a healing aspect of Animal Medicine, which comes from the ancient indigenous culture of Native American Spirituality. All creatures are honored, having characteristics that act as medicine to the two-legged ones. Octopus is a powerful sacred remedy to be called upon by men or women when needing inspiration.

**Pachamama** (sometimes written as Mama Pacha) means "Mother World" or "Mother Earth" or "Mother Land" in the language of the Quechua in South America. Pachamama is the "good mother" Goddess presiding over planting and harvesting. She is revered by the indigenous people of the Andes with a special worship day called, Martes de Challa (Challa's Tuesday). Challa is an honorary toast made to our Pachamama by spilling to Earth a small amount of a beverage before drinking it.

*PHAT!* is a sacred syllable/mantra sound that is boldly, sharply and loudly vocalized at the end of a period of silence during Vajrayana Buddhist practice. (Vajra means thunderbolt.) *PHAT!* (sometimes literally translated to mean "crack") shatters attachment to thoughts by piercing the silence, serving us in discovery of our own true natural state or Buddha Nature. A Dzogchen practitioner may sometimes lapse from vast pristine awareness becoming attached to the silence (as well as their own flowing thought-stream). Thus, the practitioner becomes a bit complacent or "lazy" in this quiet space. *PHAT!* enters to proclaim the great Dzogchen ultimate realization that ALL experience is perfect, whether there is a loud noise "interrupting" one's meditation, or not. There really is no interruption: *It is as it is.* In the bigger picture, as mystic scholar, Andrew Harvey has taught and to paraphrase him here: "...We must be careful to *not* become addicted to transcendence..." In my words (as author of this book): We develop this ultimate awareness and knowledge; mindfully realizing it without "reacting" to the sound of *PHAT!*

**Red Hat** Lineage of Tibetan Buddhism is the name for The Nyingma-pas or "The Ancient Ones" that wear very tall, ceremonial, red, crown-like pointed hats during holy empowerments before giving sacred teachings of the Buddha. Nying means heart; Nyingma-pas were the original (heart) lineage of Tibetan Buddhism, founded by the Indian Saint Padmasambhava in the Eighth Century AD. My teacher, Ven. Khenchen Palden Sherab Rinpoche was a Nyingma-pa.

**Rigpa** is a very important term in Vajrayana Buddhism, meaning intrinsic awareness, i.e., the enlightened male energy of all phenomena that penetrates the great emptiness (shunyata) as in the female womb-space.

**Scythe** is an ancient metal blade instrument used by hand to cut down tall grasses with a semi-circular sweeping motion.

**Shekinah Ruha** means Divine Feminine Spirit of God in the ancient Aramaic language. Shekinah is the feminine face of God in the Kabbalistic mystical tradition of Judaism. And in Christianity, she was once lost and is now being revitalized through a rise of the Sacred Feminine. Visit the Order of Shekinah Ruha (OSR) at: shekinahruha.org for inspiring information on the Ecumenical Spiritual Community of the Holy Spirit. (I've been a member of OSR since 2013.)

**Shofar** is a spiraling ram's horn used in sacred ceremonies of the Jewish Faith. It is blown at Yom Kippur.

**Shunyata** is a Sanskrit word; it is an important and profound term (and realization) in the Mahayana and Vajrayana Buddhist traditions. Pronounced SHOON-yah-tah, it generally means, The Great Emptiness. Here it also refers to the Divine Feminine aspect of the physical and universal womb. Consider the number zero "0" (feminine) and the number one "1" which comes after it (masculine). In the common yin/yang (dark/light) principle: shunyata is yin, the dark emptiness or cosmic womb-space that is pregnant with possibility. (See Rigpa.)

**Sky Walkers** (Skywalkers) or Sky Dancers are fearless Dakinis, the enlightened "female" spirits most important to Tibetan Buddhist practitioners. (See Dakinis.)

**Tao** means "Way" and is pronounced, DOW.

**Tara** is the essential Tibetan Buddhist Goddess of Compassion, born from the compassionate tear of Avalokiteshvara. She is the Great Mother, beloved Mother of all the Buddhas and very popular with many practitioners worldwide. There are actually 21 Tara emanations in her complete, utterly beautiful sadhana (spiritual practice). There is a Green Tara, White Tara, Black Tara, and Red Tara, etc.

**The Ten Directions** is a term of specific directions in space according to Vajrayana Buddhist teachings (originally referred to in the Lotus Sutra). The four cardinal directions are east, south, west, and north; then also, southeast, southwest, northwest, northeast, and finally augmented by, above (zenith) and below (nadir).

**The Three Times** refers to all: past, present and future. It's a term used often in Buddhist teachings.

**Tingsha** is a Tibetan word for a sacred musical instrument—two small round metal cymbals connected by a leather string. Used in Tibetan Buddhist prayer and ritual (such as sound offerings to the "hungry ghosts") Tingsha cymbals, when struck together, create a clear and high-pitched tone calling one into the present moment—"here and now." (Pronounced, TEENG-shah.)

✪

*About the Author*

Reverend Dr. Nancy Ash, DD, PhD is a heart-centered mystic and pioneering teacher of the ancient sacred ways with an integral "360" message of Oneness. Since the 1970s she's been a raja yoga therapist, energy healing conduit, sacred coach and activist.

Born in New York, she studied art at the School of Visual Arts in Manhattan before earning a BA from the University of Maryland. Ordained in 1985, Rev. Nancy is a senior interspiritual minister rooted in Dzogchen. Rev. Dr. Ash holds a Doctor of Divinity degree in metaphysics and spirituality, and was awarded a PhD in religious studies from Metropolitan University. Dr. Ash is the president of New Earth Theological University (online) netuniv.org and the dean of its School of Interspiritual Studies; and, a doctoral mentor for the ADL Ministry.

Her voice is heard worldwide as a passionate new thought leader and midwife to the new paradigm. As oversight to NewEarth University, (fractal part of the New Earth movement) she launched *Kaleidoscope,* a web TV show that inspires viewers of all ages into fresh vistas of evolutionary consciousness. Dr. Nancy Ash also serves as a Founding Trustee for the unprecedented initiative, the ITNJ at: www.itnj.org

Nancy mingles a life of service with her best friend and husband of 36 years, nestled in poetic mountains of New Mexico. She is author of the nonfiction, *Doing a 360: Turning Your Life Around to Follow Soul's Purpose,* and a poetry collection celebrating the rise of The Sacred Feminine, *Garland of Grace: Sitting with the Dying Sun.*

Dr. Ash is available for symposia panel, interviews, lectures/workshops, and spiritual direction/mentoring in-person or via phone and Skype. Browse her portal: www.Doinga360.com (scan QR code-box on back cover).

*Heartfelt Blessings to You in a Garland of Grace* ✪